THOMSON, Ruth

Musical
instruments

First published in 2007 by Franklin Watts
338 Euston Road, London NW1 3BH

Franklin Watts Australia
Level 17/207 Kent Street, Sydney NSW 2000

Copyright © Franklin Watts 2007

Design: Rachel Hamdi and Holly Fulbrook
Editor: Anne Civardi

The author would like to thank Louis Flynn and
Oliver Binks for playing the musical instruments
and Islington Education Library Service
(www.objectlessons.org) for the loan of items
from their collection.

A CIP catalogue record for this book is available
from the British Library.

Dewey Classification: 784.192

ISBN 978 0 7496 7343 7

Printed and bound in China

Franklin Watts is a division of Hachette Children's Books,
an Hachette Livre UK company.

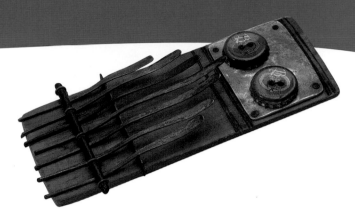

Contents

Making music 4

Bang, clack and scrape 6

Making a guiro .8

Rattle and shake 10

Making maracas 12

Jingle and tinkle 14

Making a sistrum 16

Tap and beat 18

Making a monkey drum 20

Blow away 22

Making an ocarina 24

Pluck and twang 26

Making a one-string violin 28

Handy hints 30

Glossary and index 32

A waist-belt rattle made of cocoa beans, worn for festival dances by Igbo women from south-eastern Nigeria

Cocoa beans

Making music

People everywhere make music and create musical instruments that make very different sounds.

Percussion instruments, such as drums and rattles, are either beaten or shaken. Stringed instruments, such as violins and guitars, are plucked, struck or played with a bow. Wind instruments, such as flutes and pipes, are blown to make their sound.

An Indian double pipe made from wood and a coconut shell

A South African black gourd rattle

A skin drum from Africa

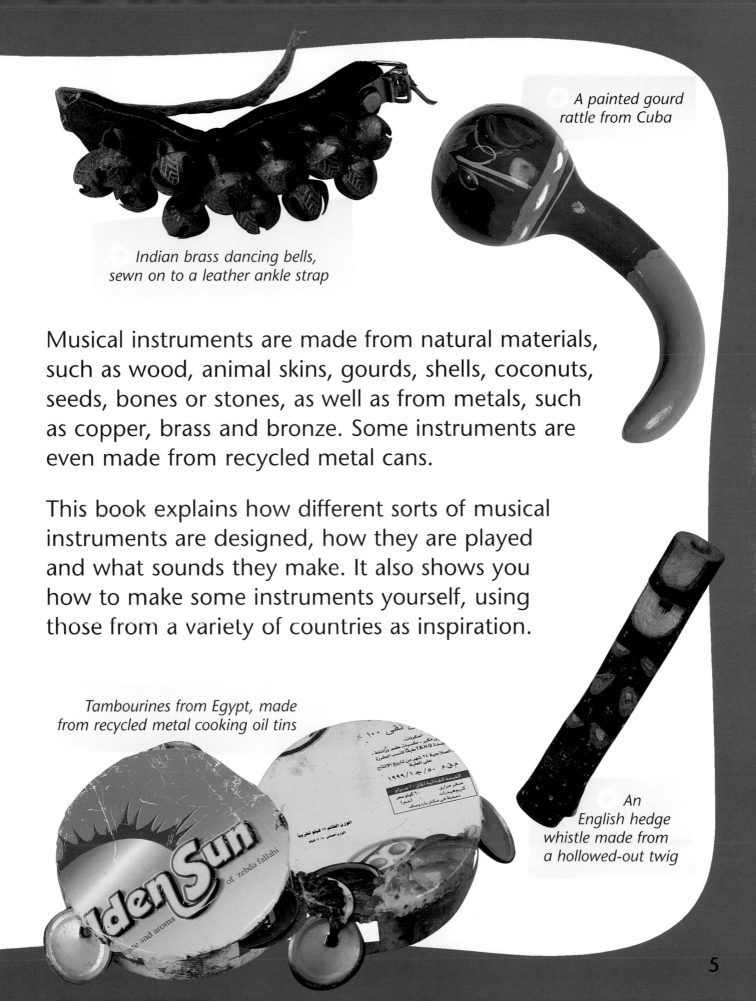

Indian brass dancing bells, sewn on to a leather ankle strap

A painted gourd rattle from Cuba

Musical instruments are made from natural materials, such as wood, animal skins, gourds, shells, coconuts, seeds, bones or stones, as well as from metals, such as copper, brass and bronze. Some instruments are even made from recycled metal cans.

This book explains how different sorts of musical instruments are designed, how they are played and what sounds they make. It also shows you how to make some instruments yourself, using those from a variety of countries as inspiration.

Tambourines from Egypt, made from recycled metal cooking oil tins

An English hedge whistle made from a hollowed-out twig

5

Bang, clack and scrape

Musicians beat or scrape percussion instruments to create rhythm. Most of the instruments have only one note, but they can be played fast or slow, loud or soft.

☀ In Cuban bands, one musician taps out the rhythm with a pair of wooden sticks called claves. He cups the hollowed-out clave in the palm of one hand and taps it with the other.

☀ Spanish flamenco dancers usually play two pairs of castanets at once. The smaller pair, which is held in the right hand, makes a higher sound than the larger ones, held in the left.

Look closer

- These castanets are carved in a hollow shell-shape.

- The two halves are joined together at the top with a cord.

- A dancer hooks her thumb through the cord. She holds the castanets against the palm of her hand and clicks them with her fingers to make a sharp, clacking sound.

Afro-Latin bands often include a musician with a guiro – a scraper made either from a hollowed-out gourd, a piece of wood or some bamboo. Guiros are scraped with either a wooden stick or a thin piece of bamboo.

☀ *This long gourd is a good shape for a guiro. It has an opening on the underside and notches along the top.*

☀ *A stick has been attached by string to this Cuban wooden guiro, so that it will not get lost.*

Look closer

- The guiros are hollow, which makes the sound louder.
- Notches have been cut all along their length.
- The stick is scraped over the notches to make a rasping sound.

Close-up of notches on a guiro

☀ *This bamboo guiro comes from Bolivia.*

1 Cut the top and base off the plastic water bottle to make a hollow tube, like this.

You will need

- a large, square-sided plastic water bottle ● scissors ● acrylic paints and a paintbrush ● corrugated card ● PVA glue ● an ice-cream stick

2 Paint the outside of the tube on all four sides. You may need to give it several coats to make the colour solid. Leave it to dry.

3 Cut any shape from corrugated card, making sure it is long and wide enough to cover the hollow tube.

4 Glue the corrugated card shape on top of the hollow tube.

PLAY THE GUIRO

Hold the guiro firmly in one hand and scrape the corrugated card rhythmically with the tip of the ice-cream stick.

Rattle and shake

African, Cuban and Brazilian musicians shake rattles to add rhythm to their lively music.

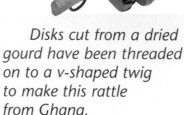

Disks cut from a dried gourd have been threaded on to a v-shaped twig to make this rattle from Ghana.

Musicians can make different sounds with a shekere. They can knock the net against the gourd, twist the gourd from side to side or pull the net taut with the twisted thread handle.

In parts of West Africa, musicians play a rattle known as a shekere. It is made from a dried, hollowed-out gourd, covered with a knotted net of shells, seeds or beads.

Look closer

- The net is open at the bottom, so it can move.
- The shells hang loosely on the threads so they can be shaken up and down.
- The hard shells knock against the hard, hollow gourd to make a loud, crisp sound.

Maracas are rattles used in Latin American music. Musicians always play them in pairs – one in each hand. The maracas are filled with seeds or dried beans, which make a swishing sound.

These wooden maracas from Cuba make different sounds – one high, the other low.

Look closer

- Maracas are round or egg-shaped, so that the seeds inside can swirl around easily and hit the sides to make a sound.

These maracas were made in Cuba. The ones above are made of papier mâché. Those on the right are made from coconut shells, which have been carved with patterns.

Making maracas

1 Blow up a balloon to the size of a large orange. Balance it on a mug with the knot on the top.

2 Cover the balloon with papier mâché (see page 30), making a ball. Let it dry. Make a second papier mâché ball exactly the same size.

3 Cut deep snips around one end of two cardboard tubes.

Open out the snips so they look like this.

12

4 When the paper balls are dry, pop the balloons. Put a handful of rice or dried beans into the balls. Cover the holes with more papier mâché.

Glue each ball on to the end of a tube, as shown. Cover them with more papier mâché to join them firmly together.

5 Paint the maracas in bright, bold colours.

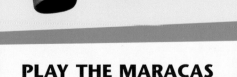

PLAY THE MARACAS

Hold the maracas upright and shake them in turn with a sharp flick of your wrist.

Metal rattles have disks strung loosely on to wire, which clink together when they are shaken. Tiny metal balls make a tinkly sound when they hit the inside of round, hollow bells.

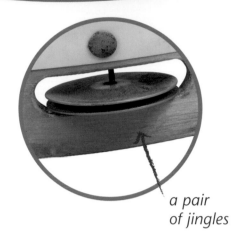

a pair of jingles

Look closer

- This tambourine has pairs of metal disks, called jingles, fitted on to rods in the slits of its frame.

Players can either shake a tambourine to make a continuous sound, or hit it sharply against their hand in time with the beat of the music.

Classical Indian dancers strap brass dancing bells, called ghungroo, around their ankles. The bells jingle in time with the steps and rhythms of the dancing.

Look closer

- Bells have been sewn in lines on to the soft, padded cloth strap of this ghungroo.
- The strap is tied just above the ankle with string.

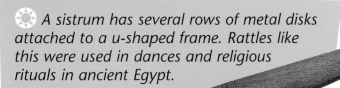

☼ *A sistrum has several rows of metal disks attached to a u-shaped frame. Rattles like this were used in dances and religious rituals in ancient Egypt.*

Look closer

- These four rattles were designed very differently, but they all have wooden handles and recycled metal jingles.

- The circular jingles are strung on to wire or nails.

☼ *This rattle from Zimbabwe has flattened metal bottle caps as jingles.*

☼ *Pairs of discarded metal bottle caps make colourful jingles for this South African shaker.*

☼ *This sistrum was made in Ghana from a forked twig, covered with fabric scraps. The jingles are made from flattened metal bottle caps.*

Making a sistrum

You will need

- a sturdy forked twig
- sandpaper • paints and a paintbrush • six metal buttons
- thin, bendy wire
- PVA varnish

1 Strip the bark off the forked twig. Sandpaper the twig to make it smooth.

2 Paint the twig a bright colour. Once the paint is dry, add some patterns. When the patterns are dry, cover the twig with a coat of varnish.

3 Thread six metal buttons on a length of thin wire. Make sure the wire is long enough to twist around both forks of the twig several times.

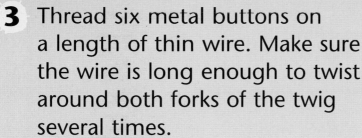

4 Twist the ends of the wire around the forks of the stick, making sure the wire is taut.

PLAY THE SISTRUM

Hold the handle firmly and jerk your wrist with short, sharp strokes to beat in time with music.

You can also shake the sistrum very fast to make a continuous jingling sound.

Tap and beat

Drums have a skin stretched tightly over a frame. When a player hits the skin with his or her hands or a beater, the skin vibrates to make a sound.

Animal skin has been stretched and sewn over a circle of wood to make this drum from Kenya.

Look closer

- All monkey drums, like these three, are double-sided.
- They are played by swivelling the handle, so that the two beads on either side click-clack alternately against the drum.

A piece of leather has been tacked on to either side of a wooden frame to make this drum.

This drum has been made from paper, stretched over a card frame.

The Indian tabla is a double instrument. Musicians play the two drums together, using their fingers and palms.

Drums are an important instrument in Indian and African music. Skilled drummers make a wide range of sounds by striking their drumskin in different places with their bare hands.

Look closer

- This djembe has been made by hollowing out a single piece of wood into the shape of a drinking goblet.

- The top is covered with goat skin.

- The skin is kept taut by cords, laced tightly in a zig-zag pattern.

tightly laced cords

The djembe originally came from West Africa, but is now played in many other parts of the world.

Making a monkey drum

1 Cut two notches opposite one another in both the base and the lid of the cheese box.

2 Cut a stick about 20cm long that fits into the notches of the box base.

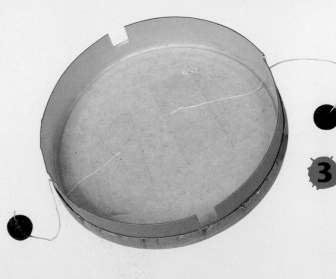

3 Cut two lengths of thread, each about 5cm long. Push one end of each thread through a bead and knot it around the bead. Tape the other end to the inside of the box base as shown.

4 Fit the stick into the notches and tape it in place. Glue around the outside edge of the box base.

Put the box lid on top. Paint the box on both sides.

PLAY THE DRUM

Hold the stick of the drum between outstretched hands, with your fingers straight. Roll the stick quickly between your palms to make the beads hit the drum.

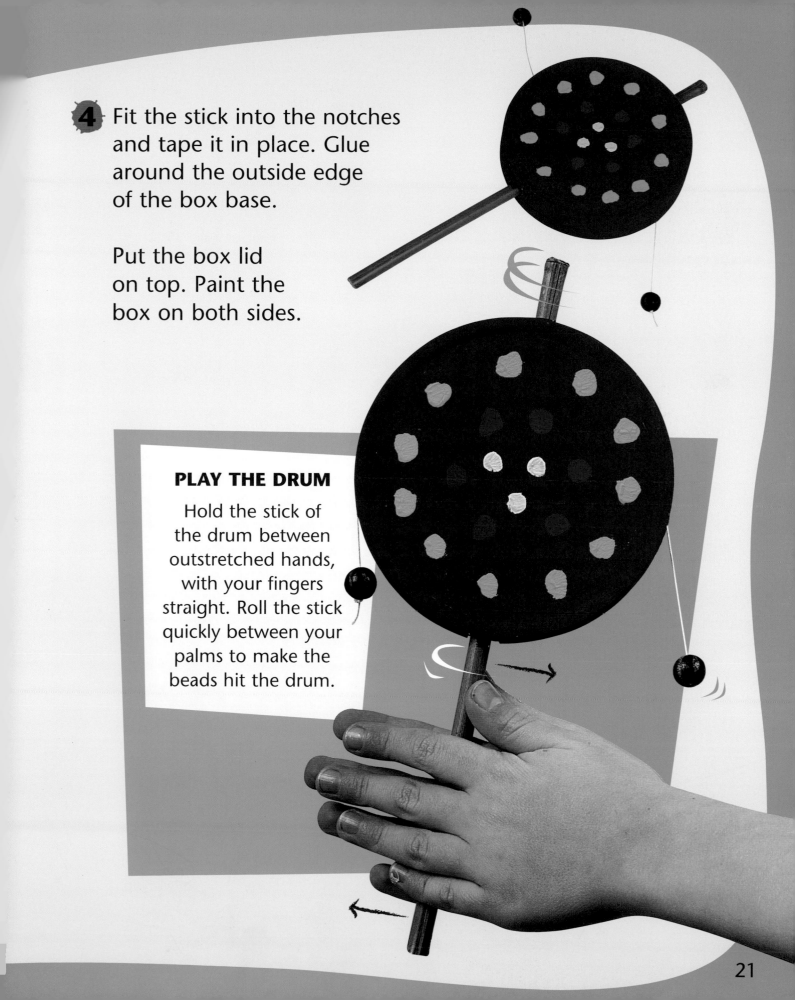

Blow away

Flutes, ocarinas and panpipes are all wind instruments. When you blow down them, the air vibrates to make sounds.

Ocarinas have holes on the top and bottom and a mouthpiece. Musicians blow through the mouthpiece and cover or uncover the holes to make different notes.

☀ Traders in the souks (markets) of Morocco, sell plastic bird whistles, like this. When the base is filled with water and the whistle is then blown, it trills just like a singing bird.

base of an ocarina

top of an ocarina

☀ These ocarinas are made of clay, which has been fired (baked hard) and glazed. Most ocarinas are egg-shaped, like this one from Peru (right). Some are made to look like animals or birds, like the two Mexican ones below.

Look closer

• The two ocarinas on the left have four finger holes. The one above has six finger holes. Both have two thumb holes on the base.

Musicians blow into or across the top of these flutes. They cover the holes with their fingertips to create different notes.

Look closer

- Both flutes are totally straight.
- They have six holes in a line, one above the other.

High in the South American Andes, musicians play panpipes – tubes made of hollow reeds, tied in a row. The pipes are closed at the bottom and musicians gently blow across the top, open end.

⚙ *People play wooden flutes called tarkas at fiestas in Peru.*

⚙ *This carved reed flute from Peru is called a kena.*

Look closer

- Panpipes have no finger holes.
- Each pipe is a different length and makes a slightly different note.

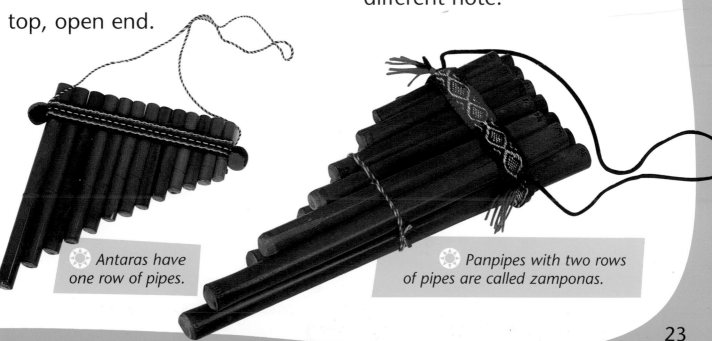

⚙ *Antaras have one row of pipes.*

⚙ *Panpipes with two rows of pipes are called zamponas.*

23

Making an ocarina

You will need

- air-drying clay ● a wooden board and rolling pin ● a mug ● a knife ● a small bowl of water ● paints and a paintbrush

1 Roll out a thin slab of clay. Use the top of a mug to cut out two circles.

2 Shape the two circles into shallow bowls, as shown.

3 Join the two bowls together (see page 31), leaving a small opening at one end.

Leave one end open.

4 Make a cube of clay small enough to fit into the opening of the ocarina. Cut a slit through its centre. This is the mouthpiece.

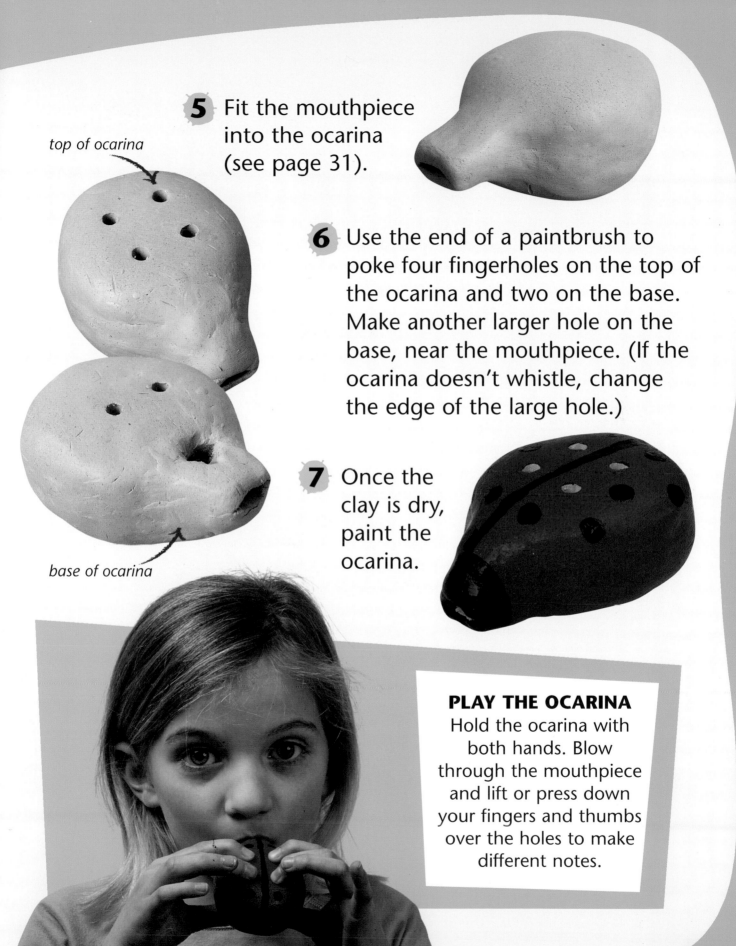

5 Fit the mouthpiece into the ocarina (see page 31).

top of ocarina

base of ocarina

6 Use the end of a paintbrush to poke four fingerholes on the top of the ocarina and two on the base. Make another larger hole on the base, near the mouthpiece. (If the ocarina doesn't whistle, change the edge of the large hole.)

7 Once the clay is dry, paint the ocarina.

PLAY THE OCARINA
Hold the ocarina with both hands. Blow through the mouthpiece and lift or press down your fingers and thumbs over the holes to make different notes.

25

Pluck and twang

When musicians play a stringed instrument, the strings vibrate to make a sound. The vibrations pass into the hollow sounding box of the instrument, which resonates (vibrates more) to make the sound louder.

peg

split cane neck

peg

☀ *The erhu is a traditional Chinese violin, played with a bow.*

☀ *The ektara from Bangladesh was once used to accompany Hindu chanting. Nowadays, it is played by folk singers, who pluck the single string with their index finger.*

Look closer

- Both the erhu *(left)* and the ektara *(right)* have only one string and a sounding box made from a coconut.

- The peg can be turned to tighten or loosen the string.

- The ektara has a split cane neck. When the two halves are squeezed together, the string becomes less taut. This lowers the sound when the string is plucked.

The mbira, a thumb piano, was first made in Zimbabwe. Musicians twang the metal keys, which are mounted on a wooden board or box, with their thumbs. A mbira can have as many as 28 keys.

☀ *These simple mbira, both from Zimbabwe, have only a few keys and were probably designed for children or as tourist souvenirs.*

Look closer

• Each key is a different length and makes a different sound.

☀ *The base of this mbira is made from a recycled tomato tin. The keys are made from sofa springs or bicycle spokes.*

• The keys are fixed firmly to a wooden board. This resonates when the keys are twanged.

• Bottle tops have been fitted on to the metal plate of the mbira above. Beads have been strung on to the keys of the one on the left. These make a buzzing sound when the keys are twanged. Buzzing is considered an essential part of the mbira sound.

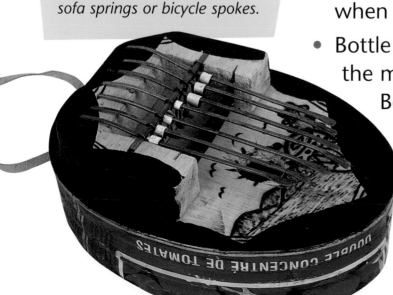

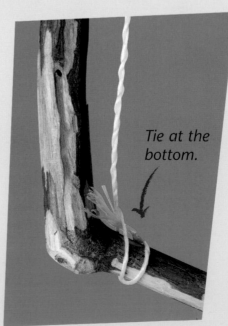

You will need

- a long, slightly curved twig
- sandpaper ● an empty plastic water bottle
- scissors ● string

1 Break off any side bits on your curved twig and smooth it all the way down its length with sandpaper.

2 Cut off the top of the water bottle.

3 Tie a length of string around the top and bottom ends of the twig, making sure the string is taut.

Tie at the top.

Tie at the bottom.

4 Loop some string over the plastic bottle. Tie the ends of the string to the bottom of the twig.

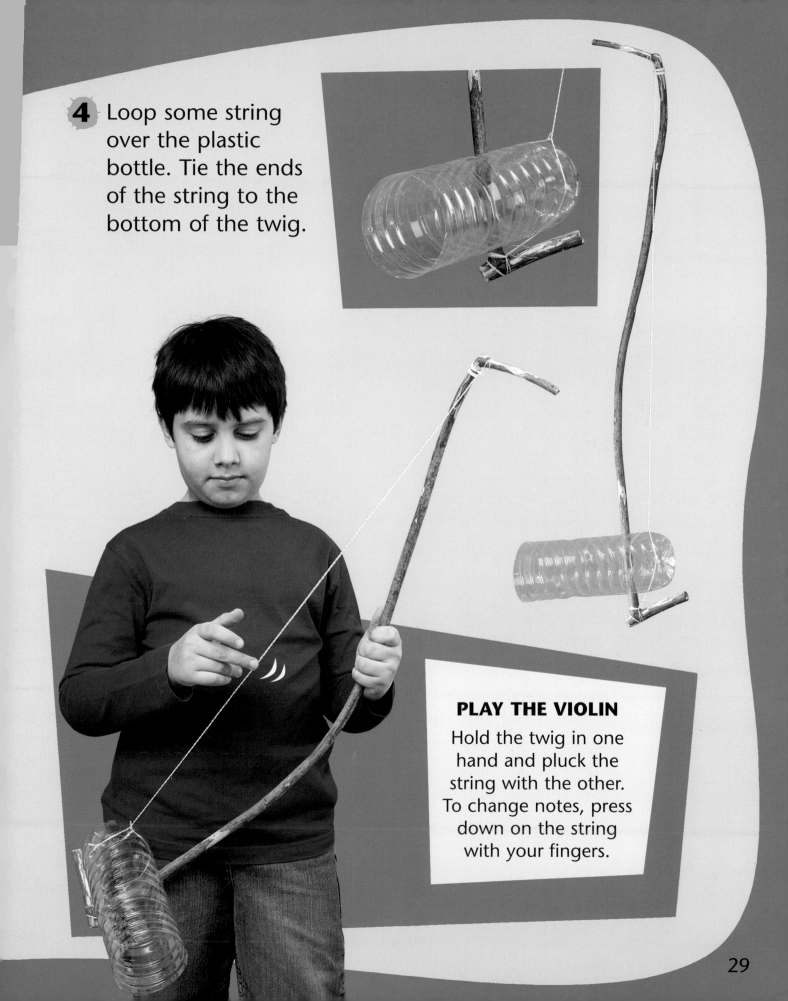

PLAY THE VIOLIN

Hold the twig in one hand and pluck the string with the other. To change notes, press down on the string with your fingers.

29

Handy hints

Making papier mâché

1 Tear newspaper into small pieces and put them into a pile. Tear pages from a colour magazine into similar pieces. Keep these in a separate pile.

newspaper pieces

magazine pieces

2 Mix PVA glue with the same amount of water in a small bowl or jug.

3 Dip the newspaper pieces into the glue mixture and overlap them all over the balloon, starting at the knot.

4 Once the balloon is covered with a layer of newspaper pieces, cover it with a layer of magazine pieces. Alternate layers of newspaper and magazine pieces until you have made seven layers altogether.

Remember: leave papier mâché to dry before painting it. It can take several days to dry completely.

Joining clay pieces together

1 Using a blunt knife, criss-cross the edges of the clay pieces you want to join.

2 Wet both edges with water and push them firmly together. Smooth the line where the pieces join, both inside and out, with your finger.

Fitting a mouthpiece into an ocarina

1 Using a blunt knife, criss-cross the clay mouthpiece on all sides. Wet it all over.

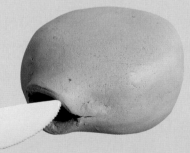

2 Using a blunt knife, criss-cross the inside of the opening of the ocarina. Wet this all over, as well.

3 Push the mouthpiece halfway into the ocarina. Press the clay of the opening firmly over the mouthpiece and smooth it.

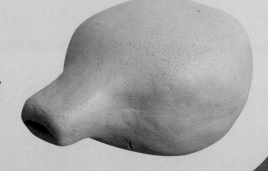

Glossary

bamboo a tall, tree-like grass with a hollow stem

beat the steady pulse of music

ceremony an event with special actions or customs that usually happen in a particular order

pluck to pull a string quickly and let it go

resonate to resound or echo

rhythm the beat of the music, which depends upon how long or short the notes are

tune to adjust an instrument so that it makes the correct sounds

vibrate to move up and down or backwards and forwards very quickly

Index

beater 18
bells 5, 14

castanets 6
claves 6

dancer
  Classical Indian 14
  Spanish flamenco 6
djembe 19
drum 4, 18–19, 20–21
drummer 19

ektara 26
erhu 26

flute 4, 22–23

ghungroo 14
gourd 4, 5, 7, 10
guiro 7, 8–9
guitar 4

instruments
  percussion 4, 6–21, 27
  recycled 5, 15, 27
  stringed 4, 26, 28–29
  wind 4, 22–23, 24–25

jingles 14, 15

kena 23
keys 27

maracas 11, 12–13
mbira (thumb piano) 27
monkey drum 18, 20–21
musicians 6, 7, 10, 11, 19, 22, 23, 26, 27

ocarina 22, 24–25, 31

panpipes 22, 23
pipe 4

rattle 4, 5, 10, 11, 14, 15

scraper 7
shaker 15
shekere 10
sistrum 15, 16–17

tabla 19
tambourine 5, 14
tarka 23

violin 4, 26, 28–29

whistle 5, 22

zampona 23